Wedding March No. I

Registration: mostly Foundation stops (for the four Wedding Marches); no Vox humana whatsoever; no research for "picturesque color"—the real "Organ" tone throughout.

42418 C

ERNEST BLOCH

FOUR WEDDING MARCHES

(with Hammond registration)

for organ

G. SCHIRMER, Inc.

DISTRIBUTED BY

HAL•LEONARD®
CORPORATION

7777 W. BLUEMOUND RD. P.O. BOX 13819 MILWAUKEE, WI 53213

6

42418

Wedding March No. II

U Bb ⑩ 00 8808 005
U Bh ⑪ 00 6888 876
L Bb ⑩ 33 8858 558
P 75

42418

42418

Wedding March No. III

U Bb (10) 00 7807 003
L Bb (10) 53 8868 568
P 86

Wedding March No. IV

(Oriental Chromatic)

U Bb ⑩ 00 6808 003
U Bb ⑪ 32 7847 333
L Bb ⑩ 53 8868 568
L Bb ⑪ 00 8876 532
P 86